Then & Now

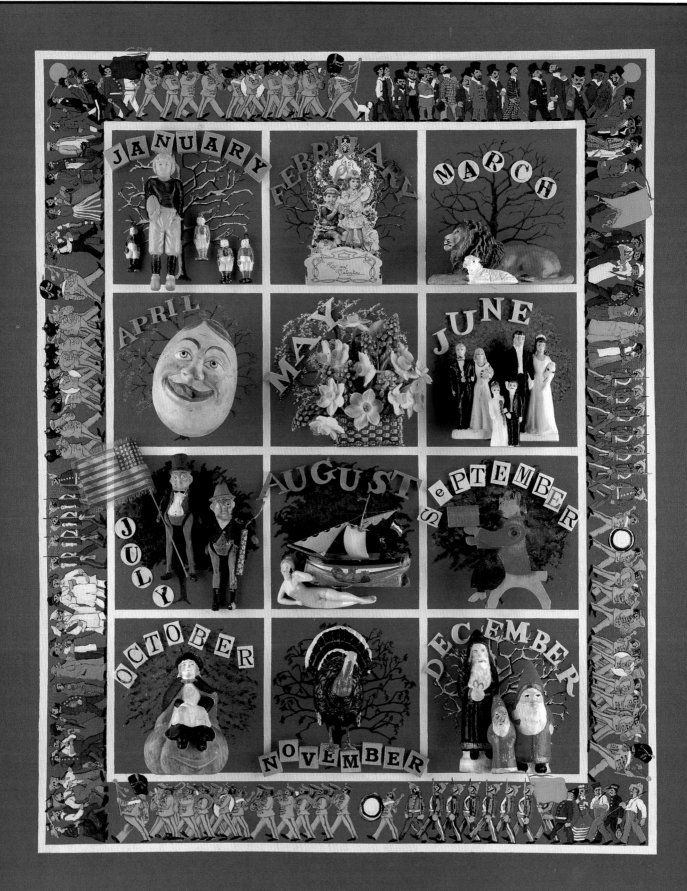

A Book of Days

Then & Now

Photographs and Text by Starr Ockenga

Painted Backgrounds by Eileen Doolittle

Houghton Mifflin Company ◆ Boston

A FLOYD YEAROUT BOOK

To Floyd,
with our thanks

Also by Starr Ockenga and Eileen Doolittle
World of Wonders, A Trip Through Numbers
The Ark in the Attic, An Alphabet Adventure

Other books by Starr Ockenga
Mirror after Mirror
Dressup: Playacts and Fantasies of Childhood

Library of Congress Cataloguing-in-Publication Data is available (#89-48631).

A FLOYD YEAROUT BOOK

X 10 9 8 7 6 5 4 3 2 1

PRINTED IN ITALY

Photographer's Note

MY BEST BIRTHDAY MEMORIES ARE FILLED WITH DAISY CROWNS, magicians, triple-dip sodas, patent leather Mary Janes, pony rides, and painted clowns. My hair had been curled in rags, and we wore ruffled party dresses. Whether it was our own party or the kid's down the block, the anticipation of the event kept us hopping from one toe to the other for days. All those memories overlap and merge into one where pink and yellow crepe paper streamers hang from the dining room chandelier, little baskets of candy with our names written on them ring the table, and noisemakers call to us from a distant past. The cake, that symbol of another year, burst through the swinging kitchen door, its candles casting a golden glow on a mother's face. "Happy Birthday to You" swelled from our young voices, usually a bit off tune.

Each year has other special events: Valentine's Day with secret love notes and bashful blushes; Easter with live chicks and bunnies and hats with long ribbons; Mother's Day and the heart-shaped lockets we bought for her at Woolworth's; weddings, when we were flower girls, bridesmaids, and then the bride; anniversaries and our own children's weddings, and the delights that sparkle through December's holiday season.

What birthday or event would be complete without the presence of a camera? Posing for a picture was part of any party. Often what we remember is that moment preserved in the album; it lives in frozen perfection. We treasure the images of our ancestors, and learn the facts of their lives through a sepia haze.

This book is about any year's array of celebrations, with something for every day. Gathered in each month's photograph, as though assembled for a group portrait, are some special people from history and contemporary culture born in that month. Those we chose to include reflect our childhood favorites. Alice, Pooh, Raggedy Ann, Ratty, and Babar are indelible. Child stars—Shirley Temple, Jackie Cooper, and Beaver—never grew up. Comic characters—Moon Mullins, Blondie and Dagwood, L'il Abner and Daisy Mae—never show a gray hair. More recent times give us new candidates—Rocky the Flying Squirrel, Clifford, Garfield, and Snoopy. And we cannot resist the anniversaries of certain inventions, like popcorn, chewing gum, and the safety pin.

In some cases, we use a symbol, an invention, or an artist's or author's creation to represent that person or event. Thus the pictures become a guessing game, with the clues provided opposite the picture. A schematic drawing with further identification is at the back of the book.

We offer this book as a jumping-off point for you to create your own book of special days. Add your family's and friend's birthdays, anniversaries, and personal landmarks on each month's pages. We include a family tree decorated with frames for you to fill with your own photographs. We also hope you will add to the cast of characters assembled: paste or tape in pictures of those dear to you. Make each month and page your own.

Happy Birthday and joy-filled occasions to each of you!

STARR OCKENGA

Before you begin, the Brownies suggest,

"Search through albums and your treasure chest.

Find the right pictures to put in these frames,

And fill in the blanks with your family's names.

The last spot in this special display

Is saved for you—because it's Your Day.

We think you'll soon be able to see

'The apple does not fall far from the tree.'"

———————

Twelve months of events make up a year;

Twelve times a crowd will assemble here.

A camera's prepared to record each face.

So get ready! Smile! And take your place!

JANUARY

Pooh, Betsy, and Alice will help to create
The spirit of January's group portrait.

1

Betsy Ross; Japanese New Year (string ball); the Rose, Cotton, and Orange Bowls; Woody Woodpecker

2

Isaac Asimov (*The Robot*)

3

Jackie Robinson; Joan Walsh Anglund ("The Lady Bug")

4

Jacob Grimm ("Little Red Riding Hood")

5

George Washington Carver

6

Joan of Arc

7

Charles Addams (Uncle Fester)

8

Elvis Presley

9

Sherlock Holmes

10

Ray Bolger (The Scarecrow)

> **BACKGROUND PAINTING:**
> *Kite Festival, Singapore*

*Date varies from year to year

> *National Diet Month*
> *Pigskin Pigout Month*

11

Banana Boat Day

12

Charles Perrault ("Sleeping Beauty")

13

Michael Bond (Paddington Bear)

14

Hugh Lofting (Dr. Doolittle and Polynesia)

15

Matthew Brady (camera); Martin Luther King

16

André Michelin (the Michelin Man); Anton Chekhov ("The Doll's House")

17

Ben Franklin (kite and key); Thomas Crapper (toilet)

18

A.A. Milne (Winnie the Pooh); Oliver Hardy; Raymond Briggs (*The Snowman*)

19

James Watts (steam engine); Robert E. Lee; Singapore Kite Festival*

20

Aquarius (Water Carrier); Harold L. Gray (Little Orphan Annie and Sandy)

21

Telly Savalas (lollipop); Super Bowl*

22

George Gordon, Lord Byron

23

John Hancock (signature)

24

California Gold Discovery Day

25

Virginia Woolf (*To the Lighthouse*)

26

Mary Mapes Dodge (Hans Brinker); Douglas MacArthur

27

Chinese New Year (dragon)*; Lewis Carroll (Alice and the Cheshire Cat)

28

Mikhail Baryshnikov

29

William McKinley

30

Franklin D. Roosevelt

31

Anna Pavlova

FEBRUARY

*As "A Token of Love" send a heart to Abe
And February's George, Clark, and the Babe.*

1

Clark Gable

2

Groundhog Day

3

Gertrude Stein

4

Russell Hoban ("The Tin Frog")

5

Hank Aaron

6

Babe Ruth

7

Charles Dickens (Scrooge and Tiny Tim); Eubie Blake (piano)

8

Boy Scouts of America anniversary; James Dean

9

Gypsy Rose Lee

10

Robert Wagner ("Hart to Hart")

11

Thomas Edison (lightbulb)

---

*National Children's Health Month
National Cherry Month*

12

Abraham Lincoln; Judy Blume (*Freckle Juice*)

13

Prince Valiant debut

14

Valentine's Day; Christopher Sholes (typewriter)

15

Charles Lewis Tiffany (jewelry bag); Susan B. Anthony; Norman Bridwell (Clifford)

16

Edgar Bergen (Charlie McCarthy); Battle of the Flowers*

17

René Laënnec (stethoscope); Marian Anderson

18

Louis Comfort Tiffany (lampshade)

19

Presidents Day (chart)*; Carson McCullers (*Clock Without Hands*)

20

Pisces (fish); Sidney Poitier ("A Raisin in the Sun"); John Glenn's orbit anniversary

21

Washington Monument anniversary; Erma Bombeck (*If Life Is Just a Bowl of Cherries, What Am I Doing in the Pits?*)

22

George Washington

23

St. George Feast Day

24

Wilhelm Grimm (Red Riding Hood's Grandma)

25

Pierre Auguste Renoir (painting)

26

Jackie Gleason; Fats Domino

27

Henry Wadsworth Longfellow

28

Milton Caniff ("Terry and the Pirates")

29

Leap Year Day; Superman

BACKGROUND PAINTING:
*Battle of the Flowers,
the South of France*

*Date varies from year to year

MARCH

Cinderella and Ratty are promised romance
Since March is a month of music and dance.

1

Glen Miller ("String of Pearls")

2

Dr. Seuss (*Green Eggs and Ham*); Mr. Rogers

3

National Anthem Day; Alexander Graham Bell
(telephone); Fontaine Fox (Toonerville Trolly)

4

Antonio Vivaldi

5

Howard Pyle (*The Wonder Clock*)

6

Michelangelo (figure of God)

7

Arbor Day/Luther Burbank; Edna A. Brown (*The
Silver Bear*)

8

Kenneth Grahame (Ratty)

9

False teeth anniversary; first soda fountain

10

Sojourner Truth; Harriet Tubman Day

| BACKGROUND PAINTING: |
| *St. Patrick's Day, Ireland* |

---

*Date varies from year to year

| *Red Cross Month* |
| *National Nutrition Month* |
| *National Peanut Month* |

11

Lawrence Welk (accordian)

12

Vaslav Nijinsky; Girl Scout anniversary

13

Discovery of Uranus

14

Albert Einstein; Hank Ketcham (Dennis the Menace)

15

Harry James (trumpet)

16

West Point anniversary (cadet)

17

St. Patrick's Day and New York Parade anniversary; Kate
Greenaway (figurine)

18

George Plimpton (*Paper Lion*); John Updike
(*Pigeon Feathers*)

19

Wyatt Earp (badge)

20

Rotten Sneaker Day

21

Aries (Ram); Johann Sebastian Bach

22

Randolph Caldecott (medal)

23

Gumby and Pokey premiere; National Bubble
Gum Week*

24

Harry Houdini (hat and rabbit)

25

Elton John (glasses)

26

Leonard Nimoy

27

Wilhelm Roentgen (X-ray)

28

Fragrance Day (lilacs)

29

Pearl Bailey (pearls)

30

Anna Sewell (*Black Beauty*); Doctor's Day

31

Andrew Lang ("Cinderella")

APRIL

April's Dagwood and Shirley seek the spotlight.
So do Jeff, Charlie, and Dudley Do-Right.

1

April Fools Day

2

First United States Mint (money); Hans Christian Andersen ("The Little Mermaid")

3

H.C. Bud Fisher (Jeff); Marlon Brando

4

Maya Angelou (*I Know Why the Caged Bird Sings*)

5

Pocahontas's Wedding Day

6

Anthony Fokker (fighter plane); Tater Day

7

William Wordsworth ("Daffodils")

8

Buddha; Catfish Hunter

9

W.C. Fields

10

Safety-pin patent anniversary; ASPCA anniversary

11

Cap Anson

Pets Are Wonderful Month

12

Easter (bunny)*; First man in space anniversary

13

Frank Woolworth (crayon); Marguerite Henry (*Misty of Chincoteague*; pony)

14

Juan Belmonte (matador); Alp Aufzug Day (goats)*

15

Leonardo da Vinci (Mona Lisa); Income Tax Day

16

Charlie Chaplin

17

Arthur Lake (Dagwood)

18

Paul Revere's ride anniversary

19

Patriot's Day (soldiers)*; Boston Marathon (runners)*

20

Taurus (bull); Bulldog Beauty Contest*

21

Charlotte Brontë (*Jane Eyre*)

22

Running of the Rodents (mice)

23

William Shakespeare; Shirley Temple Black

24

Library of Congress anniversary

25

Harold R. Garis (Uncle Wiggily)

26

Daniel Defoe (Robinson Crusoe)

27

Hugh Moore (Dixie cup); Ludwig Bemelmans (Madeline); Dudley Do-Right premiere

28

Palmer Cox (Brownie); Sham al-Nessum/Smell the Spring Day, Egypt*

29

Duke Ellington; Gideon Sundback (zipper)

30

Walpurgisnacht (witch); St. Louis Exposition opening (egg); 1939 New York World's Fair opening (pennant)

> BACKGROUND PAINTING:
> *Sham al-Nessum,*
> *"Smell the Spring," Egypt*

*Date varies from year to year

MAY

In May a top hat is the sign of Astaire,
A mouth is for "Jaws" and a flag, for Meir.

1

May Day (jonquils); Empire State Building anniversary

2

Henry McLaughlin (Clarabell); Dr. Benjamin Spock (*Feeding Your Baby and Child*)

3

Golda Meir

4

Harold Teen; Yom Ha'atzma'ut (Israeli flag)

5

Nellie Bly

6

Daniel Gerber (baby food)

7

Gary Cooper

8

Peter Benchley (Jaws)

9

James Barrie (Peter Pan and Tinkerbell); William Moulton (Wonder Woman); National Windmill Day*

10

Fred Astaire (top hat and cane)

BACKGROUND PAINTING:
National Windmill Day,
The Netherlands

*Date varies from year to year

Correct Posture Month
Garden Planting Month

11

Irving Berlin ("Easter Parade")

12

Florence Nightingale ("The Lady with the Lamp")

13

Joe Louis; Mother's Day*

14

Gabriel Daniel Fahrenheit (thermometer); WAAC founding

15

Lyman Frank Baum (*The Wonderful Wizard of Oz*); Straw Hat Day

16

Liberace (candelabra); National Cowgirl Hall of Fame anniversary

17

First Kentucky Derby (jockey)

18

First Calaveras Jumping Frog Contest

19

James Stewart (Harvey, the rabbit)

20

Dolly Madison; Charles Lindbergh ("Spirit of St. Louis")

21

Gemini (twins); Richard Shaw ("The Cat's Menu")

22

Lord Greystoke (Tarzan); Lord Olivier

23

Douglas Fairbanks

24

Frank Signorelli ("Stairway to the Stars")

25

Beverly Sills

26

Sally Ride

27

Amelia Bloomer (bloomers); Isadora Duncan

28

Dionne Quintuplets

29

Charles Strite (toaster)

30

Mel Blanc (Bugs Bunny)

31

Memorial Day (flags)*; Indianapolis 500 (race car)*

JUNE

The month of June is a royal affair,
With two little princes on a Chippendale chair.

1		**22**
	National Rose Month	
	Wedding Month	
Marilyn Monroe		Billy Wilder ("The Fortune Cookie")
2	**12**	**23**
Johnny Weismuller; Family Day*	Johanna Spyri (Heidi and her grandfather); George Bush	Duke of Windsor
3	**13**	**24**
"Casey at the Bat" anniversary	Trooping the Colour; Christo (wrapped sculpture)	First reporting of flying saucer
4	**14**	**25**
Old Maid's Day	Flag Day; Burl Ives ("The Blue Tail Fly")	Rose O'Neill (Kewpie doll)
5	**15**	**26**
Thomas Chippendale (chair); William Boyd (Hopalong Cassidy)	Smile Power Day	Abner Doubleday (baseballs)
6	**16**	**27**
First drive-in theater	Stan Laurel	Bob Keeshan (Captain Kangaroo)
7	**17**	**28**
Paul Gauguin (painting)	Father's Day*; Barney Google	Mel Brooks ("Blazing Saddles")
8	**18**	**29**
Barbara Bush	Paul McCartney	Antoine de Saint-Exupéry (*The Little Prince*)
9	**19**	**30**
Donald Duck	Moon Mullins premiere; Garfield	Charles Blondin's Niagara Falls conquest anniversary
10	**20**	
Hattie McDaniel; Judy Garland (Dorothy); Maurice Sendak (Wild Thing)	Victoria became Queen (crown)	
11	**21**	BACKGROUND PAINTING: *Trooping the Colour, Great Britain*
Jacques Cousteau ("The Golden Fish")	Cancer (crab); Martha Washington; Prince William, the Royal Heir	

*Date varies from year to year

JULY

Nancy, James Cagney, even Princess Di
Pose under the fireworks on the 4th of July.

1

Cecil Rhodes (diamonds); National Day (Canadian flag); Princess Diana

2

René Lacoste (alligator)

3

First Savings Bank

4

Independence Day (United States flag); James Bailey (circus figure)

5

P.T. Barnum

6

Beatrix Potter (Mr. Jeremy Fisher); Nancy Reagan

7

Pinocchio anniversary; Satchel Paige

8

Liberty Bell cracked; Count Ferdinand von Zeppelin (dirigible)

9

Elias Howe (sewing machine); O.J. Simpson (juice)

10

Arthur Ashe (tennis racquet)

National Hot Dog Month
July Belongs to Blueberries Month
National Hitchhiking Month

11

E.B. White (*Charlotte's Web*)

12

Bill Cosby; Different-Colored Eyes Day

13

Spud Webb

14

Bastille Day (French flag)

15

Rembrandt (painting); Clement Clark Moore (Santa and mouse)

16

District of Columbia anniversary

17

James Cagney; Ringo Starr

18

Dick Button (skater)

19

Edgar Degas (painting)

20

Moon landing anniversary

21

Frances Parkinson Keyes (*Queen Anne's Lace*); Ernest Hemingway (animal trophies)

22

Pied Piper anniversary; Margaret Williams Bianco (*The Velveteen Rabbit*)

23

Leo (lion); Pee Wee Reese

24

Alexandre Dumas (*The Three Musketeers*)

25

First flight across the English Channel (airplane)

26

Mick Jagger (stone)

27

Marci Ridlon ("A Frog Sandwich")

28

Koola Koala Birthday

29

Royal Wedding anniversary

30

Henry Ford (truck); Casey Stengel

31

John Ringling North, circus impresario (circus figures)

BACKGROUND PAINTING:
Independence Day, United States

AUGUST

A picnic in August is bound to be fun.
Join Pogo and Lucy for a romp in the sun.

1
Herman Melville (*Moby Dick*); First San Francisco cable car; National Clown Week*

2
Myrna Loy

3
John Scopes (monkey); Tony Bennett ("I Left My Heart in San Francisco"); Picnic Day, Australia*

4
Bernice Freschet ("The Ants Go Marching")

5
Neil Armstrong (astronaut)

6
Alfred, Lord Tennyson; Lucille Ball

7
Roberto Salazar (runner)

8
Andy Warhol (Campbell's Soup); Dustin Hoffman (Tootsie roll)

9
De Witt Clinton train maiden run

10
Jack Haley (the Tin Man); Soap Box Derby*

11
The Perseids ("The Night of the Shooting Stars")

> *National Vacation Month*
> *National Picnic Month*
> *Hobo Convention Month*

12
Abbott Thayer (camouflage)

13
Annie Oakley; Bert Lahr (the Cowardly Lion)

14
Rodeo in Payson, Arizona*; Magic Johnson

15
Sir Walter Scott; Allan Pinkerton (fingerprint)

16
Madonna

17
Davy Crockett

18
Meriwether Lewis (canoe)

19
Orville Wright (airplane)

20
Benjamin Harrison

21
Christopher Robin

22
Claude Debussy

23
Virgo (virgin); Lester Fine (popcorn)

24
Preston Foster (mountie)

25
Walt Kelly (Pogo Possum and Albert Alligator); Sean Connery (007)

26
Geraldine Ferraro

27
Scuba Diving Day*

28
Tasha Tudor (*The White Goose*)

29
Michael Jackson

30
Mary Wollstonecraft Shelley (Frankenstein)

31
Alan J. Lerner ("Paint Your Wagon")

> BACKGROUND PAINTING:
> *Picnic Day, Australia*

*Date varies from year to year

SEPTEMBER

Sylvester and Blondie step from a cartoon
To cheer September's Birth of the Moon.

1

Engelbert Humperdinck (*Hansel and Gretel*); Lily Tomlin ("The Incredible Shrinking Woman")

2

Eugene Field ("The Drum")

3

First "Uncle Sam"; Labor Day (laborer)*

4

Newspaper Carrier's Day (newsboy)

5

King Louis XIV (the "Sun King")

6

Claire L. Chennault (airplane)

7

Grandma Moses

8

Peter Sellers (Pink Panther); Scotch Tape anniversary

9

James Hilton (chips)

10

Arnold Palmer (golf bag)

> *Back to School Month*
> *National Sewing Month*

11

Sylvester's premiere

12

Jesse Owens; "The Monkees" premiere

13

Milton S. Hershey (chocolate bar); National Grandparents Day*

14

Ivan Pavlov (dog)

15

Penny Singleton (Blondie); Felt Hat Day

16

H.A. Rey (Curious George); Jackie Cooper; Birthday of the Moon, China*

17

William Carlos Williams ("The Red Wheelbarrow")

18

Jean Bernard Foucault (gyroscope)

19

Twiggy

20

Gus Edson (Andy Gump)

21

First ice cream cone; Great Hurricane of '38 (umbrella)

22

Postmaster General anniversary (letter carrier)

23

Libra (scale); William Holmes McGuffey (primer)

24

Jim Henson (Ernie, Oscar, and Big Bird)

25

Melville Reuben Bissell (carpet sweeper)

26

Johnny Appleseed (seeds)

27

George Cruikshank ("At the Drapers" illustration)

28

Kate Douglas Wiggin (*Rebecca of Sunnybrook Farm*); Al Capp (Li'l Abner and Daisy Mae)

29

Scotland Yard anniversary (Bobbie); Gene Autry; Rocky's premiere

30

"The Flintstones" premiere (Fred Flintstone)

> **BACKGROUND PAINTING:**
> *Birthday of the Moon, China*

*Date varies from year to year

OCTOBER

In October the scheme for spooking consumes;
Dale, Batman, and Teddy flaunt their costumes.

1

James Lawrence ("Don't give up the ship")

2

Alex Raymond (Flash Gordon); First Charlie Brown and Snoopy; Sting

3

Chubby Checker

4

St. Francis of Assisi (doves); Ten-Four Day

5

Robert Hutchings (rocket)

6

Brown Paper Bag Day

7

James Whitcomb Riley

8

Chicago Fire anniversary (Mrs. O'Leary's cow and lantern); Captain Edward Rickenbacker; Fire Prevention Week (fireman and ladder)*

9

John Lennon

10

U.S. Naval Academy anniversary (midshipman); Helen Hayes

11

"Leave It to Beaver" premiere

Pizza Festival Month
National Pasta Month

12

Columbus Day*

13

United States Navy Day (sailor)

14

Dwight D. Eisenhower; Lois Lenski (*The Little Fire Engine*)

15

Evangelista Torricelli (barometer); Oktoberfest in Germany*

16

"Happy Birthday to You" copyright date (cake)

17

Evel Knievel (stuntman)

18

Mason-Dixon Line established

19

Sweetest Day (mints)

20

Bela Lugosi (Dracula)

21

Alfred B. Nobel (dynamite)

22

Franz Lizst

23

Scorpio (scorpion); Pele (soccer ball)

24

Robert Kane (Batman and Robin); United Nations anniversary (flag)

25

Pablo Picasso (child with dove)

26

Joseph Hansom (carriage)

27

Teddy Roosevelt; Emily Post (white gloves); Enid Bagnold (*The Chalk Garden*)

28

Statue of Liberty anniversary

29

Make Your Halloween Costume Day (box with scissors)

30

Ted Williams

31

Halloween (skeleton); John Keats ("Ode on a Grecian Urn"); Dale Evans

BACKGROUND PAINTING:
Oktoberfest, Bavaria

*Date varies from year to year

NOVEMBER

Mark Twain and Mickey concocted a plan
For November's gang to parade in Japan.

1

Mexico Day of the Dead (skeletons); Stephen Crane (*Red Badge of Courage*)

2

Daniel Boone (coonskin hat); Steve Ditko (Spiderman)

3

John Montague, Earl of Sandwich

4

Will Rogers; Discovery of King Tut's Tomb (mummy)

5

Roy Rogers

6

Adolph Sax (saxophone); James Naismith (basketball)

7

Madame Curie

8

Katherine Hepburn

9

Ed Wynn; Kay Thompson (*Eloise*)

10

Oliver Goldsmith ("The Bee")

BACKGROUND PAINTING:
Shichi-Go-San, Japan

Harvest Month

11

Abigail Adams

12

Princess Grace

13

Robert Louis Stevenson (Long John Silver); Nathaniel Benchley ("A Ghost Named Fred")

14

Prince Charles

15

Georgia O'Keeffe (skull); Shichi-Go-San, Japan*

16

George S. Kaufman ("Solid Gold Cadillac")

17

Homemade Bread Day

18

Mickey Mouse; Alan Shepard (astronaut)

19

George Rogers Clark (canoe)

20

Chester Gould (Dick Tracy and Junior)

21

Harpo Marx

22

Charles de Gaulle

23

Sagittarius (archer); Billy the Kid

24

Frances Hodgson Burnett (*The Secret Garden*)

25

Joe DiMaggio

26

Thanksgiving Day (turkey; football corsage)*

27

Johnny Marks ("Rudolph the Red-Nosed Reindeer")

28

William Blake ("Tiger, tiger, burning bright")

29

C.S. Lewis (*The Lion, the Witch and the Wardrobe* and *The Silver Chair*)

30

Samuel Langhorne Clemens (Mark Twain)

*Date varies from year to year

DECEMBER

"To December! Our holiday jamboree!"
Toast Raggedy, Popeye, and little ET.

1

Cyril Ritchard (Captain Hook)

2

Margaret Hamilton (Wicked Witch of the West); Peter Goldmark (color television)

3

Joseph Conrad

4

Monroe Leaf (Ferdinand)

5

Walt Disney (Dumbo)

6

St. Nicholas Day; Joyce Kilmer ("Trees")

7

Mary, Queen of Scots

8

C.G. Segar (Popeye)

9

Joel Chandler Harris (Brer Rabbit); Jean de Brunhoff (Babar)

10

Karl von Drais (bicycle); "Mighty Mouse" TV premiere

11

UNICEF anniversary

| *Holiday Festivities Month* |

12

Katzenjammer Kids anniversary

13

Phillips Brooks ("O Little Town of Bethlehem")

14

South Pole discovery (dogsled); Raggedy Ann

15

Chanukah (menorah)*; Alexandre Gustave Eiffel (tower)

16

Posadas, Mexico (piñatas); Ludwig von Beethoven; Boston Tea Party (crate)

17

John Greenleaf Whittier

18

Joseph Grimaldi (clown); First giant panda in U.S.; Steven Spielberg (ET)

19

Underdog Day (Dr. Watson); National Whiner's Day (baby)

20

Harvey S. Firestone (button)

21

Chester Greenwood Day, Maine (earmuffs)

22

Capricorn (goat); Sebastian Bauer (submarine)

23

Trim-a-Tree Day

24

Christmas Eve (Santa Claus); Kit Carson

25

Christmas (Christ Child); Clara Barton; Humphrey Bogart

26

Boxing Day (presents); *Mayflower* landing

27

Howdy Doody

28

William Semple (chewing gum)

29

Charles Goodyear (blimp)

30

Asa Griggs Chandler (Coca-Cola)

31

New Year's Eve (streamers); Monopoly game patent anniversary

> **BACKGROUND PAINTING:**
> *Posadas, Mexico*

*Date varies from year to year

NOTES

NOTES

JANUARY

★National Diet Month; ★★Pigskin Pigout Month

DATE	YEAR	EVENT
1a	1752	Betsy Ross, patriot; reputed to have made the first American flag at the request of George Washington.
1b		Japanese New Year.
1c		The Rose, Cotton, and Orange Bowl games, collegiate football playoffs.
1d	1941	Woody Woodpecker, cartoon character; created by Walter Lantz.
2	1920	Isaac Asimov, author and biochemist.
3a	1919	Jackie Robinson, first black baseball player to play with a major league team.
3b	1926	Joan Walsh Anglund, poet.
4	1785	Jacob Grimm, German mythologist and author.
5	1864	George Washington Carver death anniversary; agricultural scientist, author, teacher, inventor.
6	1412	Joan of Arc, French heroine, who led a small army that forced the British to leave Orleans.
7	1912	Charles Addams, cartoon artist, creator of "The Addams Family."
8	1935	Elvis Presley, "The King," singer, composer, and rock star.
9	1854	Sherlock Holmes, British detective; created by Sir Arthur Conan Doyle
10	1904	Ray Bolger, actor; portrayed Scarecrow in "The Wizard of Oz."
11		Banana Boat Day, invention of the banana split.
12	1628	Charles Perrault, French author and mythologist; first recorder of fairy tales.
13	1926	Michael Bond, British author; creator of Paddington Bear.
14	1886	Hugh Lofting, author; creator of Dr. Doolittle.
15a	1823	Matthew Brady, Civil War photographer.
15b	1929	Martin Luther King, civil rights leader.
16a	1853	André Michelin, French tire manufacturer.
16b	1860	Anton Chekhov, Russian playwright.
17a	1706	Benjamin Franklin, scientist, diplomat, author, publisher, philanthropist.
17b	1910	Thomas Crapper death anniversary; prime developer of modern flush toilet (born ca. 1837).
18	1882	A.A. Milne, British author, creator of Winnie the Pooh.
18b	1892	Oliver Hardy, actor and comedian.
18c	1934	Raymond Briggs, British author.
19a	1736	James Watts, inventor.
19b	1807	Robert E. Lee, Civil War Confederate general.
19c		Kite Festival, Singapore.*
20a		Zodiac sign of Aquarius, the Water Carrier, 1/20–2/19.
20b	1894	Harold L. Gray, cartoonist, creator of "Little Orphan Annie."
21a		Super Bowl, professional championship football playoffs, 3rd Sunday in January.*
21b	1926	Telly Savalas, actor.
22	1788	George Gordon, Lord Byron, British Romantic poet.
23	1727	John Hancock, patriot and statesman; first signer of the Declaration of Independence; basis of expression "Put your John Hancock here." Also, National Handwriting Day.
24	1848	Gold discovered at Sutter's Mill, CA.
25	1882	Virginia Woolf, British author.
26a	1831	Mary Mapes Dodge, author of *Hans Brinker and the Silver Skates*.
26b	1880	Douglas MacArthur, World War II and Korean War general.
27a		Chinese New Year.*
27b	1832	Lewis Carroll (C.L. Dodgson), British author, *Alice's Adventures in Wonderland*.
28	1948	Mikhail Baryshnikov, ballet dancer.
29	1843	William McKinley, 25th President.
30	1882	Franklin D. Roosevelt, 32nd President.
31	1882	Anna Pavlova, Russian ballerina.

*Date varies from year to year

FEBRUARY

★National Children's Health Month;
★★National Cherry Month

DATE	YEAR	EVENT
1	1901	Clark Gable, actor; portrayed Rhett Butler in "Gone with the Wind."
2	1887	Groundhog Day; if the groundhog sees his shadow, he returns to his burrow for another six weeks of winter; Punxsutawney, PA.
3	1874	Gertrude Stein, author.
4	1925	Russell Hoban, poet.
5	1934	Hank Aaron, "Homerun King," baseball player.
6	1895	Babe Ruth (George Herman Ruth), "The Sultan of Swat," baseball player.
7a	1812	Charles Dickens, British author, *A Christmas Carol.*
7b	1883	Eubie Blake, composer and jazz pianist.
8a	1910	Boy Scouts of America, founded in Washington, D.C., by William Baden Powell.
8b	1931	James Dean, actor.
9	1914	Gypsy Rose Lee (Rose Louise Lee), actress, entertainer.
10	1930	Robert Wagner, actor, starred in TV series "Hart to Hart."
11	1847	Inventors Day, celebrated on birthday of Thomas Edison, who invented incandescent electric lamp, phonograph, movie camera, telephone transmitter.
12a	1809	Abraham Lincoln, "Honest Abe," 16th President.
12b	1938	Judy Blume, author.
13	1937	"Prince Valiant" first appeared; created by Harold Foster, Canadian cartoonist (born 8/16/1892).
14a		Valentine's Day.
14b	1819	Christopher Latham Sholes, inventor of the typewriter.
15a	1812	Charles Lewis Tiffany, jeweler.
15b	1820	Susan Brownell Anthony, reformer, advocate of women's suffrage and temperance abolitionist.
15c	1928	Norman Bridwell, author, *Clifford, The Big Red Dog.*
16a	1903	Edgar Bergen, actor, radio entertainer, and ventriloquist; voice of Charlie McCarthy.
16b		Battle of the Flowers, France; celebrated with floats, parades, and flowers thrown in the streets.*
17a	1781	René Laënnec, French physician, author, and inventor of the stethoscope.
17b	1902	Marian Anderson, opera singer.
18	1848	Louis Comfort Tiffany, artist, glassmaker, created iridescent "favrile" glass.
19a		President's Day, celebrated on the 3rd Monday in February.*
19b	1917	Carson McCullers, author.
20a		Zodiac sign of Pisces, the Fish, 2/20–3/20.
20b	1927	Sidney Poitier, actor.
20c	1962	John Glenn, orbited earth in *Friendship* 7.
21a	1885	Washington Monument dedication anniversary.
21b	1927	Erma Bombeck, author, humorist.
22	1732	George Washington, "Father of Our Country," 1st President.
23	A.D. 303	St. George Feast Day, martyr and patron saint of England, death anniversary. Legend says St. George's faith helped him slay the dragon, which had demanded the sacrifice of the king's daughter.
24	1786	Wilhelm Grimm (brother of Jacob), German mythologist and author of "Little Red Riding Hood."
25	1841	Pierre Auguste Renoir, French artist; pictured: "Girl with Watering Can."
26a	1916	Jackie Gleason, "The Great One," actor, starred in TV series "The Honeymooners."
26b	1928	Fats Domino, jazz musician.
27	1807	Henry Wadsworth Longfellow, poet.
28	1907	Milton Caniff, cartoonist, created "Terry and the Pirates."
29a		Leap Year Day (occurs every four years); people born this day have one-fourth fewer birthdays.
29b	1938	Superman, comic character; born on Krypton; created by Jerome Siegal and Joe Shuster.

*Date varies from year to year

MARCH

DATE	YEAR	EVENT
1	1904	Glen Miller, bandleader, composer, and trombonist.
2a	1904	Dr. Seuss (Ted Geisel), author and illustrator.
2b	1928	Mr. Rogers (Fred Rogers), entertainer, TV series "Mr. Rogers' Neighborhood."
3a	1931	National Anthem Day, "Star Spangled Banner," written by Francis Scott Key (born 8/1/1779).
3b	1842	Alexander Graham Bell, inventor of the telephone.
3c	1884	Fontaine Fox, creator of "Toonerville Folks" (1915).
4	1678	Antonio Vivaldi, Italian baroque composer.
5	1853	Howard Pyle, illustrator of children's books.
6	1475	Michelangelo (Michelangelo Buonarroti), Italian Renaissance artist; painted the Sistine Chapel.
7a	1849	Arbor Day, in honor of Luther Burbank, naturalist and author, creator and developer of many new varieties of fruit, flowers, trees, and vegetables.
7b	1875	Edna A. Brown, author.
8	1859	Kenneth Grahame, British author, *The Wind in the Willows.*
9a	1822	Patent granted to Charles Graham for the first false teeth.
9b	1858	First soda fountain established in Lowell, MA.
10a	1797	Sojourner Truth, abolitionist and civil rights leader.
10b	1813	Harriet Tubman Day, death anniversary; abolitionist, Underground Railroad leader, called "Moses of Her People."
11	1903	Lawrence Welk, "The Polka King," bandleader and accordian player.
12a	1890	Vaslav Nijinsky, Russian ballet dancer.
12b	1912	Anniversary of founding of Girl Scouts of America by Juliette Gordon Low.
13	1781	Planet Uranus discovered by Sir William Herschel, British astronomer.
14a	1879	Albert Einstein, American physicist.
14b	1920	Hank Ketcham, cartoonist; created "Dennis the Menace."
15	1916	Harry James, bandleader and trumpet player.
16	1802	United States Military Academy established at West Point, NY.
17a	A.D. 493	St. Patrick's Day; patron saint of Ireland; National Day of Ireland.
17b	1762	First St. Patrick's Day Parade in New York City.
17c	1846	Kate Greenaway, British author.
18a	1927	George Plimpton, author.
18b	1932	John Updike, author.
19	1848	Wyatt Earp, Western frontier lawman.
20		Rotten Sneaker Day.
21a		Zodiac sign of Aries, the Ram, 3/21–4/19.
21b	1685	Johann Sebastian Bach, German composer and organist.

DATE	YEAR	EVENT
22	1846	Randolph Caldecott, British artist and illustrator, after whom the Caldecott Medal for children's book illustrations is named.
23a	1957	"Gumby and Pokey" premiered on TV.
23b		National Bubble Gum Week.*
24	1874	Harry Houdini, Hungarian magician and escape artist.
25	1947	Elton John, British musician and rock star.
26	1931	Leonard Nimoy, actor; portrayed Mr. Spock in "Star Trek."
27	1845	Wilhelm Roentgen, German scientist; discovered X-rays (11/8/1895).
28		Fragrance Day.
29	1918	Pearl Bailey, jazz and blues singer, actress.
30a	1820	Anna Sewell, author.
30b	1933	Doctor's Day established to honor doctors with the symbol of the red carnation, on the day that Dr. Crawford W. Long became the first physician to use ether as an anesthetic (3/30/1842).
31	1844	Andrew Lang, author and mythologist, *The Blue Fairy Book.*

*Date varies from year to year

APRIL

★*Pets Are Wonderful Month*

DATE	YEAR	EVENT
1		April Fool's Day or All Fools' Day.
2a	1792	First United States Mint established at Philadelphia, PA.
2b	1805	Hans Christian Andersen, Danish author.
3a	1885	H.C. Bud Fisher, cartoonist; creator of "Mutt and Jeff."
3b	1924	Marlon Brando, actor.
4	1928	Maya Angelou, poet.
5	1614	Pocahontas married John Rolfe.
6a	1890	Anthony Fokker, German airplane manufacturer.
6b		Salute to the sweet potato.
7	1770	William Wordsworth, English Lakes poet and philosopher.
8a	563 B.C.	Hana Matsuri (Flower Festival), Japan; commemorates Buddha's birthday.
8b	1946	James "Catfish" Hunter, baseball pitcher.
9	1879	W.C. Fields, actor and expert juggler.
10a	1849	Patent for safety pin granted to Walter Hunt of New York City.
10b	1886	American Society for the Prevention of Cruelty to Animals founded.
11	1851	Adrian "Cap" Anson, baseball player.
12a		Easter, Christian holiday celebrating the resurrection of Jesus Christ.★
12b	1961	Yuri Gagarin became first man in space; orbited the earth in 108 minutes in *Vostok I*.
13a	1852	Frank Woolworth, merchant.
13b	1902	Marguerite Henry, author.
14a	1892	Juan Belmonte, Spanish matador.
14b		Alp Aufzug, "Ascent"; herdsmen throughout the Alps lead their goats up to mountain pastures. Celebrates the beginning of spring.★
15a	1452	Leonardo da Vinci, Italian Renaissance artist, inventor, and architect.
15b		Internal Revenue Service income tax filing deadline.
16	1889	Charles "Charlie" Chaplin, actor and comedian.
17	1905	Arthur Lake, actor; portrayed Dagwood in "Blondie."
18	1775	Paul Revere's ride anniversary.
19a	1775	Patriot's Day, anniversary of Battle of Lexington and Concord; opening volleys of the American Revolution; celebrated in Mass. and Me. the 3rd Monday of April.★
19b		Boston Marathon; oldest marathon in America, run on Patriot's Day.★
20a		Zodiac sign of Taurus, the Bull, 4/20–5/20.
20b		Drake Bulldog Beauty Contest, Des Moines, IA.★
21	1816	Charlotte Bronte, British author.
22		Running of the Rodents; naming of Mr. and Mrs. Rodent, Louisville, KY.
23a	1564	William Shakespeare, British poet and playwright.

23b	1928	Shirley Temple Black, child actress and currently diplomat.
24	1800	Library of Congress established.
25	1873	Howard R. Garis, author and creator of Uncle Wiggily.
26	1661	Daniel Defoe, British author.
27a	1887	Hugh Moore, inventor of disposable paper cup (in 1908).
27b	1898	Ludwig Bemelmans, French author.
27c	1969	Dudley Do-Right premiered on TV.
28a	1840	Palmer Cox, author and creator of the "Brownies."
28b		Sham al-Nessum, "Smell the Spring Day," Egypt; observed by all sects and religions. Families go on picnics in the country, usually with brightly colored eggs.
29a	1899	Duke Ellington, composer and pianist.
29b	1913	Zipper patented by Gideon Sundback, employee of Hook and Eye Company, Hoboken, NJ.
30a		Walpurgisnacht, Europe. For centuries people believed witches rode through the sky on the eve of May Day (St. Walpurga's Day).
30b	1904	St. Louis Exposition opened.
30c	1939	New York World's Fair opened.

★Date varies from year to year

MAY

★Correct Posture Month; ★★Garden Planting Month

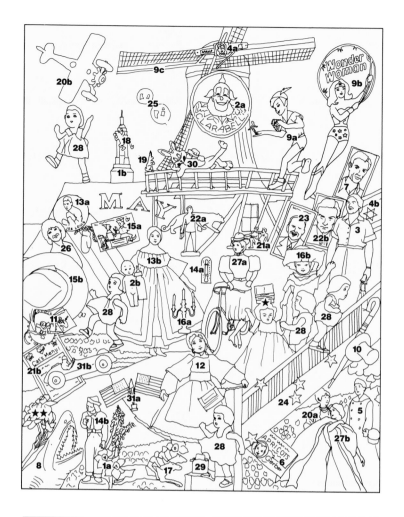

DATE	YEAR	EVENT
1a		May Day; spring holiday since ancient times.
1b	1931	Empire State Building opened as the tallest building in the world.
2a	1893	Henry McLaughlin, actor, portrayed Clarabell on "Howdy Doody."
2b	1903	Benjamin Spock, pediatrician and author.
3	1898	Golda Meir, Israeli Prime Minister.
4a	1919	Harold Teen, cartoon character, introduced; created by Carl Ed (born 7/16/1890).
4b	1948	Yom Ha'atzma'ut, Israeli Independence Day; establishment of Provisional Government of Israel.
5	1867	Nellie Bly (Elizabeth Corcoran), journalist and women's rights advocate.
6	1898	Daniel Gerber, baby food manufacturer.
7	1901	Gary Cooper, actor.
8	1940	Peter Benchley, author of *Jaws*.
9a	1860	James Barrie, Scottish playwright and author, *Peter Pan*.
9b	1983	William Moulton, cartoonist; creator of "Wonder Woman."
9c		National Windmill Day, The Netherlands; held 2nd Saturday in May.★
10	1899	Fred Astaire, actor, dancer, singer.
11	1888	Irving Berlin, songwriter.
12	1820	Florence Nightingale, British nurse and public health activist.
13a	1914	Joe Louis (Joseph Louis Barrow), World Heavyweight Boxing Champion 1937–1949.
13b		Mother's Day, held 2nd Sunday in June.
14a	1681	Gabriel Daniel Fahrenheit, German physicist, introduced mercury into thermometers.
14b	1942	Congress established the Womens' Auxiliary Army Corps.
15a	1856	Lyman Frank Baum, newspaperman and author.
15b		Men start wearing straw hats for the summer.
16a	1919	Liberace, pianist.
16b	1975	National Cowgirl Hall of Fame and Western Heritage established, Hereford, TX.
17	1875	First Kentucky Derby, American's premier horse race; now held 1st Saturday in May.
18	1928	First Calaveras Jumping Frog Contest, a reenactment of Mark Twain's story; Angel's Camp, CA.
19	1908	James "Jimmy" Stewart, actor, starred in "Harvey."
20a	1768	Dolly Madison, wife of James Madison, 4th President.
20b	1927	Charles Lindbergh flight anniversary; first solo transatlantic flight.
21a		Zodiac sign of Gemini, the Twins, 5/21–6/20.
21b	1923	Richard Shaw, poet.
22a	1888	Lord Greystoke, model for Edgar Rice Burroughs' Tarzan.
22b	1907	Sir Laurence Olivier, British actor.
23	1883	Douglas Fairbanks, actor.
24	1901	Frank Signorelli, composer.
25	1929	Beverly Sills, opera singer, impresario.
26	1951	Sally Ride, astronaut, first woman in space.
27a	1818	Amelia Jenks Bloomer, pioneer in feminism; promoted bloomers as sensible dress for women.
27b	1878	Isadora Duncan, interpretive dancer.
28	1934	The Dionne Quintuplets.
29	1919	Charles Strite, inventor of the pop-up toaster.
30	1908	Mel Blanc, voice of Bugs Bunny and many other comic characters.
31a	1865	Memorial Day (Decoration Day), established for honoring those who have died in battle; held last Monday in May.★
31b		Indianapolis 500 car race, held last Saturday in May.★

★Date varies from year to year

JUNE

★National Rose Month; ★★Wedding Month

DATE	YEAR	EVENT
1	1926	Marilyn Monroe, actress.
2a	1904	Johnny Weissmuller, swimmer, actor.
2b		Family Day, the 1st Sunday in June.*
3	1888	Mighty Casey Has Struck Out anniversary; "Casey at the Bat" first appeared in *San Francisco Examiner;* written by Ernest L. Thayer.
4		Old Maid's Day
5a	1718	Thomas Chippendale, British cabinetmaker.
5b	1895	William Boyd, western actor; portrayed Hopalong Cassidy.
6	1933	First drive-in theater opens, Camden, NJ; invented by Richard M. Hollingshead, Jr.
7	1848	Paul Gauguin, French artist; pictured: "The Moon and the Earth."
8	1925	Barbara Bush, wife of George Bush, 41st President.
9	1934	Donald Duck, Walt Disney cartoon character.
10a	1895	Hattie McDaniel, actress; played Mammy in "Gone with the Wind."
10b	1922	Judy Garland, actress and singer; portrayed Dorothy in "The Wizard of Oz."
10c	1928	Maurice Sendak, author and illustrator, *Where the Wild Things Are.*
11	1910	Jacques Cousteau, French marine explorer.
12a	1827	Johanna Spyri, Swiss author, *Heidi.*
12b	1924	George Bush, 41st President.
13a	1775	Trooping the Colour, England; the official Queen's Birthday Parade; held on a Saturday in June.*
13b	1935	Christo, artist and sculptor.
14a	1887	Flag Day established to honor the "Stars and Stripes," which became the American flag in 1777.
14b	1909	Burl Ives, actor and singer.
15		Smile Power Day.
16	1890	Stan Laurel, actor and comedian.
17a		Father's Day, 3rd Sunday in June.*
17b	1919	Barney Google introduced by Billy De Beck, cartoonist (born 4/15/1890).
18	1942	Paul McCartney, British musician and rock star; a Beatle.
19a	1923	Moon Mullins first appeared; created by Frank Willard, cartoonist (born 9/21/1893).
19b	1978	Garfield, cartoon character; created by Jim Davis (born 7/28/1945).
20	1837	Queen Victoria ascended to the British throne.
21a		Zodiac sign of Cancer, the Crab, 6/21–7/22.
21b	1732	Martha Washington, wife of George Washington, 1st President.
21c	1982	Prince William of Wales, son of Prince Charles and Princess Diana; heir to the British throne.
22	1906	Billy Wilder, film director.

DATE	YEAR	EVENT
23	1894	Duke of Windsor, Edward VIII, British monarch who gave up his throne for American divorcee Wallis Simpson.
24	1947	First Flying Saucer Reported anniversary; sighted by Kenneth Arnold over Mt. Rainier, WA.
25	1874	Rose O'Neill, dollmaker and creator of Kewpie dolls.
26	1819	Abner Doubleday, originator of the game of baseball.
27	1927	Bob Keeshan, actor.
28	1926	Mel Brooks, film director and comedian.
29	1900	Antoine de Saint-Exupéry, French author and aviator.
30	1859	Charles Blondin's Conquest of Niagara Falls anniversary; French acrobat and aerialist walked across Niagara Falls on a tightrope before a crowd of 25,000 people.

*Date varies from year to year

JULY

★National Hot Dog Month;
★★July Belongs to Blueberries Month;
★★★National Hitchhiking Month

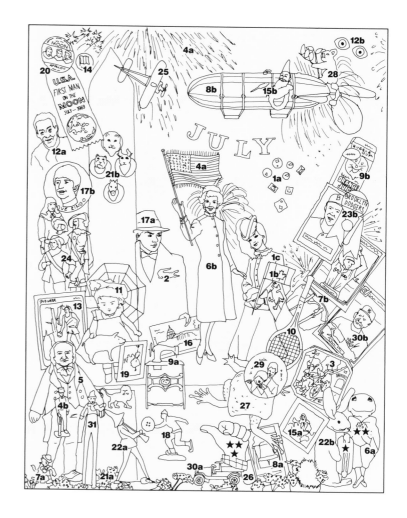

DATE	YEAR	EVENT
1a	1853	Cecil John Rhodes, English-born South African millionaire-politician. Reputed to have controlled 90% of the world's diamond production at one time. Founded the Rhodes Scholarships.
1b	1867	National Day, Canada; commemorates the confederation of Upper and Lower Canada and some of the Maritime Provinces into the Dominion of Canada.
1c	1961	Princess Diana, wife of Prince Charles.
2	1905	René Lacoste, French tennis player and sports clothing manufacturer.
3	1819	First Savings Bank opened in New York City.
4a	1776	United States Independence Day; Declaration of Independence was signed at Philadelphia, PA.
4b	1847	James A. Bailey, circus impresario.
5	1810	P.T. Barnum, circus impresario.
6a	1886	Beatrix Potter, British author and illustrator; creator of numerous animal characters.
6b	1923	Nancy Reagan, wife of Ronald Reagan, 40th President.
7a	1881	"Pinocchio" published in "Children's Journal of Rome," authored by Carlo Collodi (born 11/24/1826).
7b	1906	Satchel Paige, baseball player.
8a	1835	Liberty Bell cracks, Philadelphia, PA.
8b	1838	Count Ferdinand von Zeppelin, German inventor of the dirigible (first flight 7/20/1900).
9a	1819	Elias Howe, inventor of the sewing machine.
9b	1947	O.J. Simpson, football player, sportscaster.
10	1943	Arthur Ashe, first black tennis player to be named to the American Davis Cup Team.
11	1899	E.B. White, author.
12a	1936	Bill Cosby, actor, comedian, and author.
12b		Celebrates uniqueness of people with two different-colored eyes, Southampton, PA.
13	1963	"Spud" Webb, basketball player.
14	1749	Bastille Day, France, commemorates the fall of the Bastille at the beginning of the French Revolution.
15a	1606	Rembrandt van Rijn, Dutch artist; pictured: "Woman Cutting Her Nails."
15b	1823	Clement Clark Moore, author and teacher.
16	1790	District of Columbia anniversary; established as the permanent capital of the United States.
17a	1899	James Cagney, actor.
17b	1940	Ringo Starr, British rock singer, a Beatle.
18	1929	Dick Button, Olympic figure skater and sportscaster.
19	1834	Edgar Degas, French artist; pictured: "Dancer on Stage."
20	1969	Anniversary of man's first landing on the moon.
21a	1885	Frances Parkinson Keyes, author and poet.
21b	1889	Ernest Hemingway, author and hunter.
22a	1376	Pied Piper of Hamelin anniversary. Pied Piper piped the rats out of Hamelin at the request of the townspeople. When he was not paid, he piped the children out of town, never to be seen again.
22b	1881	Margery Williams Bianco, author.
23a		Zodiac sign of Leo, the Lion, 7/23–8/22.
23b	1919	Harold "Pee Wee" Reese, baseball player.
24	1802	Alexandre Dumas, French author.
25	1909	Louis Blériot, French aviator, flew from Calais, France to Dover, England (born 7/1/1872).
26	1943	Mick Jagger, British rock star, member of the Rolling Stones.
27	1942	Marci Ridlon, poet.
28		Koola Koala Birthday, celebrates the first magical Koala. "Make a wish, place it in Koala's magic pouch, and it will come true."
29	1981	Prince Charles married Lady Diana Spencer.
30a	1863	Henry Ford, automotive pioneer.
30b	1891	Casey Stengel, baseball player and manager of the New York Mets and the New York Yankees.
31	1903	John Ringling North, circus impresario.

*Date varies from year to year

AUGUST

★National Vacation Month; ★★National Picnic Month;
★★★ Hobo Convention Month

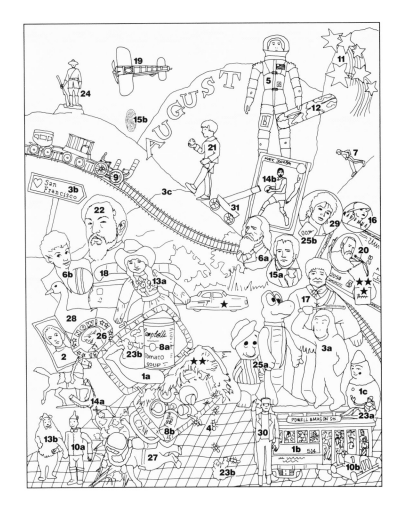

DATE	YEAR	EVENT
1a	1819	Herman Melville, author.
1b	1873	First cable car in San Francisco; introduced by Andrew Smith Hallide.
1c		National Clown Week, Woodlynne, NJ.*
2	1905	Myrna Loy, actress, portrayed Nora Charles in "The Thin Man."
3a	1900	John Scopes, biology teacher and central figure in the "Scopes Monkey Trial," convicted for teaching evolution theory.
3b	1926	Tony Bennett, singer.
3c		Picnic Day, Australia.*
4	1927	Bernice Freschet, author.
5	1930	Neil Armstrong, astronaut.
6a	1809	Alfred, Lord Tennyson, British poet.
6b	1911	Lucille Ball, actress and comedienne.
7	1959	Roberto Salazar, marathon runner.
8a	1930	Andy Warhol, pop artist and film director.
8b	1937	Dustin Hoffman, actor, starred in "Tootsie."
9	1831	*De Witt Clinton* train made its maiden run from Albany to Schenectady, NY in 46 minutes; 3rd public carrier in the United States to operate under steam.
10a	1899	Jack Haley, actor, portrayed the Tin Man in "The Wizard of Oz."
10b		All-American Soap Box Derby, Akron, OH. First Derby founded in 1934 by news photographer Myron Scott in Dayton, OH.*
11		The Perseids, an annual meteor shower that appears to originate in the constellation Perseus.
12	1849	Abbott Handerson Thayer, discoverer of camouflage.
13a	1860	Annie Oakley, markswoman; starred in Buffalo Bill's Wild West Show.
13b	1895	Bert Lahr, actor and comedian, portrayed the Cowardly Lion in "The Wizard of Oz."
14a	1884	World's Oldest Continuous Rodeo, Payson, AZ.*
14b	1959	Earvin "Magic" Johnson, basketball player.
15a	1771	Sir Walter Scott, Scottish poet and author.
15b	1819	Allan Pinkerton, detective and founder of detective agency; first chief of United States Army's Secret Service.
16	1958	Madonna (Louise Ciccone), rock singer and actress.
17	1786	Davy Crockett, frontiersman.
18	1774	Meriwether Lewis, explorer; co-leader of Lewis and Clark Expedition.
19	1871	Orville Wright, aviation pioneer; piloted first self-powered flight. Also celebrated as National Aviation Day (since 1939).
20	1833	Benjamin Harrison, 23rd President.
21	1920	Christopher Robin, British inspiration for "Pooh" stories.
22	1862	Claude Debussy, French musician and composer.
23a		Zodiac sign of Virgo, the Virgin, 8/23–9/22.
23b	1916	Lester L. Fine, inventor of popcorn.
24	1902	Preston Foster, actor, portrayed the Mountie.
25a	1913	Walt Kelly, cartoonist, creator of "Pogo."
25b	1930	Sean Connery, British actor; portrayed James Bond in the film series.
26	1935	Geraldine Ferraro, first woman to be nominated as United States vice-presidential candidate.
27		Scuba Diving Day.*
28	1915	Tasha Tudor, author and illustrator.
29	1958	Michael Jackson, rock star.
30	1797	Mary Wollstonecraft Shelley, British poet and author.
31	1918	Alan J. Lerner, playwright and lyricist.

*Date varies from year to year

SEPTEMBER
★Back to School Month; ★★National Sewing Month

DATE	YEAR	EVENT
1a	1854	Engelbert Humperdinck, composer, *Hansel and Gretel*.
1b	1939	Lily Tomlin, actress and comedienne.
2	1850	Eugene Field, poet; known as the "Children's Poet."
3a	1813	The first recorded use of the term Uncle Sam in print; *Troy Post*.
3b		Labor Day; 1st Monday in September.*
4	1833	Commemorates hiring of first newsboy in the United States; 10-year-old Barney Flaherty, by *the New York Sun*.
5	1638	Louis XIV, French monarch.
6	1890	Claire L. Chennault, aviator for the Air Force; formed American flying group called "Flying Tigers" to give aid to China in its war with Japan.
7	1860	Grandma Moses (Anna Mary Robertson), artist.
8a	1925	Peter Sellers, British actor.
8b	1930	Scotch Tape, first introduced by the Minnesota Mining and Manufacturing Company; invented by Richard G. Drew.
9	1900	James Hilton, British author of *Goodbye, Mr. Chips*.
10	1929	Arnold Palmer, golfer.
11	1976	"Sylvester" premiered on television.
12a	1813	Jesse Owens, track star.
12b	1966	"The Monkees" premiered on television.
13a	1855	Milton S. Hershey, candy manufacturer.
13b	1979	National Grandparents Day; celebrated the Sunday following Labor Day.*
14	1849	Ivan Pavlov, Russian physiologist and animal behaviorist.
15a	1908	Penny Singleton, actress; portrayed Blondie.
15b		Felt Hat Day; men resume wearing winter hats.
16a	1898	H.A. Rey, author, creator of Curious George.
16b	1922	Jackie Cooper, actor.
16c		Birthday of the Moon, China, mid-autumn festival. Legend states that the Old Man in the Moon ties couples together with red silk thread. Moon is the fullest and brightest of the year.*
17	1883	William Carlos Williams, poet.
18	1819	Jean Bernard Foucault, French inventor of gyroscope.
19	1949	Twiggy (Leslie Hornby), British model and actress.
20	1901	Gus Edson, cartonist, creator of "The Gumps."
21a	1903	Ice cream cone birthday. Italo Marchiony created a cone for holding ices: patent granted 12/15/1903.
21b	1938	Great Hurricane anniversary.
22	1789	Office of Postmaster General established.
23a		Zodiac sign of Libra, the Balance, 9/23–10/22.
23b	1800	William Holmes McGuffey, educator and author.
24	1936	Jim Henson, muppeteer.
25	1843	Melville Reuben Bissell, inventor, with his wife, Anna, of the carpet sweeper.

26	1774	Johnny Appleseed (John Chapman), planter of orchards, friend of wild animals; regarded by Indians to be a great medicine man.
27	1792	George Cruikshank, British illustrator.
28a	1856	Kate Douglas Wiggin, author.
28b	1909	Al Capp, cartoonist; creator of "Li'l Abner."
29a	1829	Scotland Yard established; Greater London's metropolitan police, known as "Bobbies."
29b	1907	Gene Autry, the "Singing Cowboy," western actor, baseball impresario.
29c	1959	"Rocky and His Friends" premiered on television.
30	1960	"The Flintstones" premiered on television.

*Date varies from year to year

OCTOBER

★Pizza Festival Month; ★★National Pasta Month

DATE	YEAR	EVENT
1	1781	James Lawrence, naval officer, whose dying words became a naval motto: "Don't give up the ship."
2a	1909	Alex Raymond, cartoonist; creator of "Flash Gordon."
2b	1950	The "Peanuts" gang was created by Charles M. Schultz (born 11/26/1922).
2c	1951	Sting (Gordon Sumner), actor and rock star.
3	1941	Chubby Checker (Ernest Evans), entertainer, twister.
4a	1811	St. Francis of Assisi, Italian religious and spiritual leader.
4b		Ten-Four Day; day of recognition for radio operators, whose code word "ten-four" signifies an affirmative reply; 4th day of 10th month.
5	1882	Robert Hutchings, "Father of the Space Age," pioneer of rocket propulsion.
6	1845	Charles Stilwell, inventor of the brown paper bag.
7	1853	James Whitcomb Riley, Hoosier poet.
8a	1871	Great Fire of Chicago anniversary; caused by Mrs. O'Leary's cow kicking over a lantern in a barn on DeKoven Street.
8b	1890	Edward Rickenbacker, aviator, auto racer, war hero.
8c	1925	Fire Prevention Week; to advocate the need for fire prevention; a week in early October that includes the date of the Great Chicago Fire.*
9	1940	John Lennon, British rock star, composer, singer; a Beatle.
10a	1845	United States Naval Academy opened in Annapolis, MD.
10b	1900	Helen Hayes, actress.
11	1957	Premiere of "Leave It to Beaver," starring Jerry Mathers.
12	1492	Columbus Day; commemorates Christopher Columbus's arrival in the Bahamas; observed 2nd Monday in October.*
13	1775	United States Navy established by legislation passed by the Second Continental Congress.
14a	1890	Dwight D. Eisenhower, "Ike," 34th President.
14b	1893	Lois Lenski, author.
15a	1608	Evangelista Torricelli, Italian inventor of the barometer.
15b		Oktoberfest, Bavaria; festival celebrating harvest.*
16	1893	"Happy Birthday to You" copyrighted by two sisters, Mildred Hill (born 1859), who composed the melody, and Patty Smith Hill (born 1868), who wrote the lyrics.
17	1938	Evel Knievel, daredevil.
18	1767	Mason-Dixon Line settled.
19		Sweetest Day; to celebrate friendship by giving sweets.
20	1888	Bela Lugosi, actor, portrayed Dracula.
21	1833	Alfred B. Nobel, Swedish chemist and inventor of dynamite; established the Nobel Prize.
22	1811	Franz Liszt, Hungarian composer.
23a		Zodiac sign of Scorpio, the Scorpion; 10/23–11/22.
23b	1940	Pele, Brazilian soccer player.
24a	1916	Robert Kane, cartoonist; creator of "Batman."

24b	1945	Founding of the United Nations.
25	1881	Pablo Picasso, Spanish artist; detail pictured: "Child with Dove."
26	1803	Joseph Hansom, British architect and inventor of the Hansom cab.
27a	1858	Theodore Roosevelt, 26th President.
27b	1872	Emily Post, author on manners; *Etiquette: The Blue Book of Social Usage.*
27c	1889	Enid Bagnold, British author of *The Chalk Garden.*
28	1886	Statue of Liberty anniversary; created by Frédéric Auguste Bartholdi, French sculptor.
29		Make Your Halloween Costume Day.
30	1918	Ted Williams, baseball player.
31a		Halloween.
31b	1795	John Keats, British poet.
31c	1912	Dale Evans, western actress.

Date varies from year to year

NOVEMBER
★Harvest Month

DATE	YEAR	EVENT
1a		Mexico Day of the Dead; departed souls are remembered with joy and feasting; also All Saints Day.
1b	1871	Stephen Crane, author.
2a	1734	Daniel Boone, frontiersman, pioneer, guide.
2b	1927	Steve Ditko, cartoonist, creator of "Spiderman."
3	1718	John Montague, Fourth Earl of Sandwich, after whom the sandwich is named.
4a	1879	Will Rogers, humorist, actor, author.
4b	1922	King Tut's Tomb discovered at Luxor, Egypt, by British archaeologist Howard Carter.
5	1912	Roy Rogers, western actor.
6a	1814	Adolph Sax, Belgian musician and inventor of the saxophone.
6b	1861	James Naismith, inventor of the game of basketball.
7	1867	Marie Curie, Polish chemist and physicist; discovered radioactivity.
8	1909	Katherine Hepburn, actress.
9a	1886	Ed Wynn, actor and comedian.
9b	1912	Kay Thompson, author.
10	1728	Oliver Goldsmith, English author and poet.
11	1744	Abigail Adams, wife of John Adams, 2nd President.
12	1929	Princess Grace of Monaco, born Grace Kelly.
13a	1850	Robert Louis Stevenson, Scottish author, *Treasure Island*.
13b	1915	Nathaniel Benchley, author.
14	1948	Prince Charles, heir to the British throne.
15a	1887	Georgia O'Keeffe, artist; detail pictured: "Cow's Skull—Red, White, and Blue."
15b		Shichi-Go-San, Japan; "7-5-3" celebrates all children who are 7, 5 and 3. Dressed in kimonos, they go to a shrine with their families carrying paper bags with good luck signs. Priests drop "1000 year" candies into the bags.*
16	1889	George S. Kaufman, playwright.
17		Homemade Bread Day.
18a	1920	Mickey Mouse, Walt Disney cartoon character.
18b	1923	Alan Shepard, astronaut, first American in space.
19	1752	George Rogers Clark, explorer; co-leader of Lewis and Clark Expedition.
20	1900	Chester Gould, cartoonist, creator of "Dick Tracy."
21	1893	Harpo Marx, comedian.
22	1890	Charles de Gaulle, French general and president.
23a		Zodiac sign of Sagittarius, the Archer, 11/23–12/21.
23b	1859	Billy the Kid, outlaw.
24	1849	Frances Hodgson Burnett, author.
25	1914	Joe DiMaggio, baseball player.

DATE	YEAR	EVENT
26a	1789	President George Washington proclaimed fourth Thursday in November to be Thanksgiving. Commemorates first Thanksgiving, held in 1621.*
26b		Thanksgiving Day football games.*
27	1909	Johnny Marks, author, songwriter.
28	1757	William Blake, British poet, "The Tiger."
29	1878	C.S. Lewis, British author and poet.
30	1835	Samuel Langhorne Clemens (Mark Twain), author.

Date varies from year to year

DECEMBER
★*Holiday Festivities Month*

DATE	YEAR	EVENT
1	1898	Cyril Ritchard, British actor.
2a	1903	Margaret Hamilton, actress; performed in "The Wizard of Oz."
2b	1906	Peter Carl Goldmark, inventor of color television.
3	1857	Joseph Conrad, British author.
4	1905	Monroe Leaf, author.
5	1901	Walt Disney, animated-film pioneer.
6a		St. Nicholas' Day; bishop of Myra in 4th century, noted for his charity. Santa Claus and giving of gifts is said to have derived from him. Patron saint of children.
6b	1886	Joyce Kilmer, poet.
7	1542	Mary, Queen of Scots.
8	1894	C.G. Segar, creator of "Popeye."
9a	1848	Joel Chandler Harris, American author, wrote "Uncle Remus" series.
9b	1897	Jean de Brunhoff, French author, creator of Babar.
10a	1851	Karl von Drais, German inventor, "Father of the Modern Bicycle," death anniversary; born 1784; patented two-wheel riding machine in 1818.
10b	1955	"Mighty Mouse" premiered on television.
11	1946	United Nations International Children's Emergency Fund established.
12	1897	"Katzenjammer Kids" first appeared in *American Humorist;* created by Rudolph Dirks, cartoonist.
13	1835	Phillips Brooks, clergyman and composer; wrote the lyrics for "O Little Town of Bethlehem."
14	1911	South Pole discovered by Roald Amundsen, Norwegian explorer, with 4 companions and 52 sled dogs.
14b	1914	Raggedy Ann, created by Johnny Gruelle.
15a		Chanukah, Feast of Lights or Feast of Dedication; commemorates victory of Maccabees over Syrians and the rededication of the Temple at Jerusalem; lasts 8 days.*
15	1832	Alexandre Gustave Eiffel, French engineer; designed Eiffel Tower.
16a		Posadas, Mexico. For each of the 8 nights before Christmas, Mexicans reenact Joseph and Mary's search for shelter (*posadas*) on the night before Jesus's birth. Celebrated with piñatas filled with toys and candy.
16b	1770	Ludwig von Beethoven, German composer and conductor.
16c	1773	Boston patriots boarded British ships in the Boston Harbor and dumped nearly 350 chests of tea into the water.
17	1807	John Greenleaf Whittier, poet.
18a	1778	Joseph Grimaldi, British clown; known as "Greatest Clown in History," "King of Clowns."
18b	1936	First giant panda exported to the U.S. from China.
18c	1947	Steven Spielberg, film producer, director.
19a		Underdog Day; celebrates underdogs and unsung heroes (like Dr. Watson and Friday); 3rd Friday in December.*
19b		National Whiner's Day.
20	1868	Harvey S. Firestone, founder of Firestone Tire and Rubber.
21		Chester Greenwood Day in Maine; celebrates the inventor of the earmuff, invented in 1873; patented in 1877.
22a		Zodiac sign of Capricorn, the Goat, 12/22–1/19.
22b	1822	Sebastian Bauer, inventor and builder of submarines.
23		Trim-a-Tree Day.
24a		Christmas Eve; traditionally Santa Claus brings toys to good little girls and boys.
24b	1809	Kit Carson, frontiersman and scout.
25a		Christmas; celebrates the birth of the Christ Child.
25b	1821	Clara Barton, nurse and founder of the American Red Cross.
25c	1899	Humphrey Bogart, actor.
26a		Boxing Day, Britain, Christmas gift "boxes" traditionally given to postman, dustman, and other tradespeople.
26b	1620	Pilgrims landed in Plymouth, MA, in *Mayflower.*
27	1947	Howdy Doody, television character.
28	1869	William F. Semple, of Mt. Vernon, OH, granted patent for chewing gum.
29	1900	Charles Goodyear, inventor and developer of vulcanized rubber used in tires.
30	1851	Asa Griggs Chandler, developer of Coca–Cola.
31a		New Year's Eve.
31b	1935	Monopoly game patented by Parker Brothers Games, invented by Charles B. Darrow.

*Date varies from year to year

Acknowledgments

WE ARE GRATEFUL to The Children's Museum of Indianapolis, especially to Peter V. Sterling, executive director, and Paul K. Richard, deputy director of exhibits and programs, for their support and generous loan of artifacts; to curators Bob Johnson, Bob Pickering, Mary Jane Tetters-Eichacker, Judi Ryan, and Vallorie Alsup for guiding us through the collections; to collections management staff Robin Lipp, Ron Gibson, Terri Ridgeway, and Ben Brackett for retrieval and shipping.

We thank Roberta Batt and Mary Donaldson of Pekl; Dorene Burger and Stacey Potenzano of Antiques by Dorene, Inc., Ray and Gennie Fleming, Marion and Jerry Harris, Donald Hillman and Stephen Weiss of Hillman Gemini, Eileen and Hugh Kavanagh, Chip and Blair Parker; Kathy Parker; Inger Kynaston; the Maxon children; Jocelyn Ritter; Lark Ryan; Noah Ryan; Elaine Skinner of Mostly Paper; the Steele boys; Grover van Dexter of Second Childhood, who helped in our search for small objects and who opened their collections to us; Christopher Isenberg for his advice on sports figures and the use of his cards; the United States Historical Society, especially Martha Gibby, for lending us the dolls, Abigail Adams, Marion Anderson, Nellie Bly, Isadora Duncan, Dolly Madison, Grandma Moses, and Betsy Ross; the artisans who created figures and objects for us: Karen Brent for Alice and the Cheshire Cat, Christopher Robin, Peter Pan and Tinkerbell, and the Koala Bear; Douglas Darracott for paper pieces; Judi Ryan for the Velveteen Rabbit; Susan Sirkis for Cinderella; Diane Smoler for Sleeping Beauty and Florence Nightingale; and Ted Stetkewicz for Matthew Brady's camera.

We deeply appreciate the continued efforts of our "team"—Bill Wright for his technical assistance and good humor through the photographing sessions; Susan Marsh for her book design that enhances the spirit of our work; Mary Reilly for the charm and delicacy of her schematic drawings; Floyd Yearout for his guidance, expertise, and nurturing; and Walter Lorraine at Houghton Mifflin for his enthusiasm to publish *Then & Now*.

Bibliography

Burnett, Bernice, *Holidays, A First Reference Book*. New York: Franklin Watts, 1984.

Caney, Steven. *Steven Caney's Invention Book*. New York: Workman Publishing, 1985.

Carruth, Gorton. *The Encyclopedia of American Facts and Dates*. New York: Harper and Row, Publishers, 1987.

Chase, William D. and Helen M. *Chase's Annual Events*. Chicago: Contemporary Books, Inc., 1987.

Daiches, David, Bradbury, Malcolm, and Mottram, Eric. *The Avenel Companion to English and American Literature*. New York: Avenel Books, 1981.

Daniel, Clifton. *Chronicle of the 20th Century*. New York: Chronicle Publishing, 1987.

de Montrieville, Doris, and Crawford, Elizabeth D. *The 4th Book of Junior Authors and Illustrators*. New York: The H.W. Wilson Company, 1978.

Dodge, Ellen. *You Are Your Birthday*. New York: Simon and Schuster, Inc., 1986.

Horn, Maurice. *World Encyclopedia of Comics*. New York: Chelsea House Publishers, 1976.

Leigh, Matthew Andrew. *The Birthmate Book*. Toronto: Paperjacks, Ltd., 1988.

Lucaire, Ed. *The Celebrity Book of Lists*. New York: Stein and Day, 1985.

McWhirter, Norris. *The Guinness Book of World Records*. New York: Bantam Books 1985.

Merriam-Webster. *Webster's New Biographical Dictionary*. Springfield, MA: Merriam-Webster, 1988.

Panati, Charles. *The Extraordinary Origins of Everyday Things*. New York: Harper and Row, Publishers, 1987.

Schlesinger, Arthur M., Jr. *The Almanac of American History*. New York: Putnam Publishing Company, 1983.

Terrace, Vincent. *The Complete Encyclopedia of Television Programs, 1947-1979*. New York: A.S. Barnes and Company, Inc., 1979.

Wallechinsky, David, and Wallace, Irving. *The People's Almanac #3*. Toronto: Bantam Books, 1981.

van Straalen, Alice. *The Book of Holidays Around the World*. New York: E.P. Dutton, 1986.

Vare, Ethlie Ann, and Ptacek, Greg. *Mothers of Invention*. New York: William Morrow and Company, Inc., 1988.

DESIGNED BY SUSAN MARSH

SCHEMATICS DRAWN BY MARY REILLY

TYPE SET IN GALLIARD BY MONOTYPE COMPOSITION COMPANY

PRODUCTION COORDINATED BY TRILOGY · PRINTED BY MAZZUCCHELLI · MILAN · ITALY